PARTS OF ME

A SERIES OF UNTAMED WORDS

RITUPARNA ROUTH

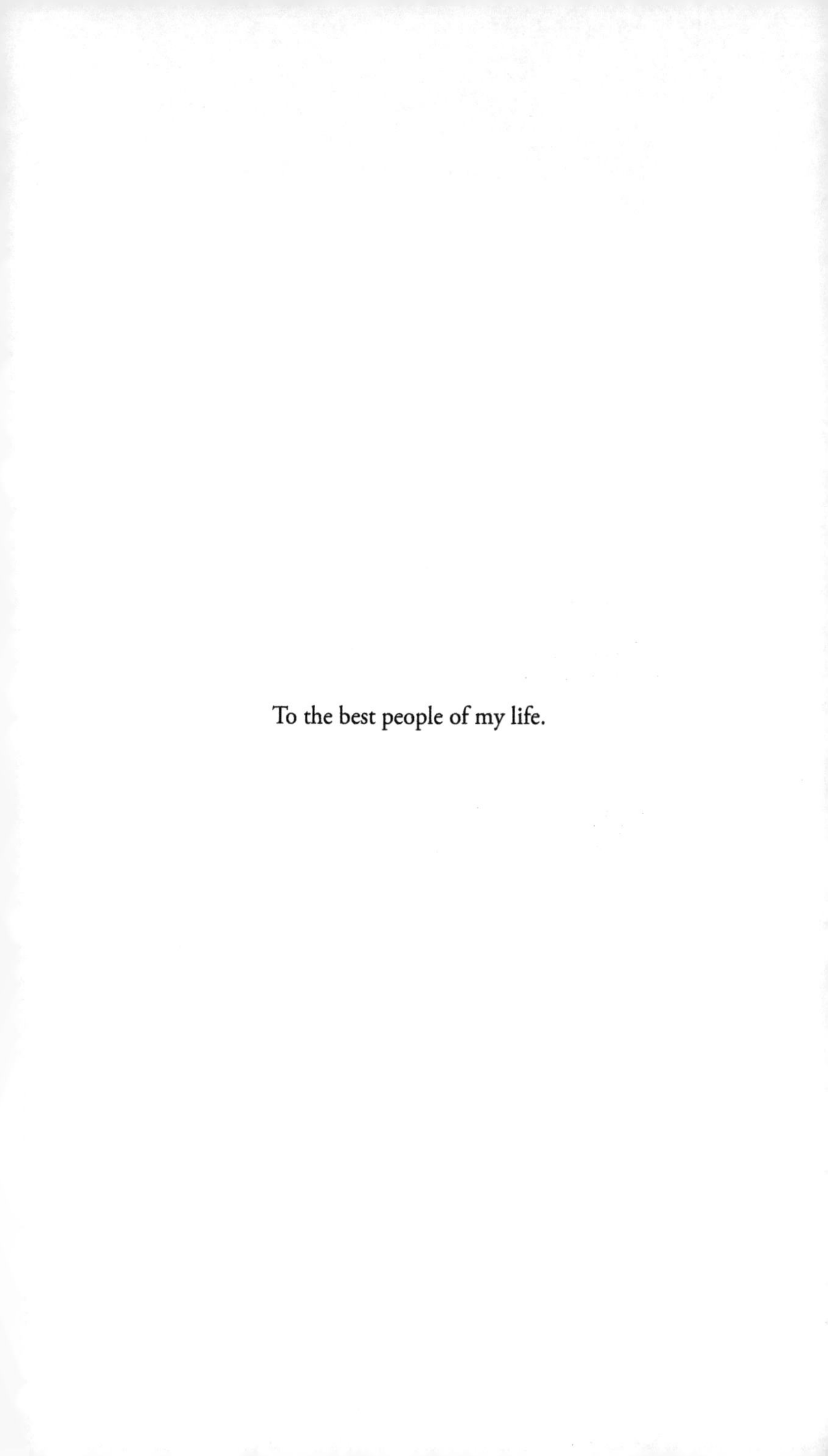

To the best people of my life.

Contents

Contents

Foreword

This book is a roller-coaster ride through every human emotion. Parts of Me hits all the right spots and lets you devour life with ease. This book discusses grief, beauty, and reality through words.

Preface

Parts Of Me: A series of untamed words is a tribute to every human out there. It explores humans through their overwhelming emotions and uncontrollable words.

Acknowledgements

This book is solely dedicated to my family. Thank you for never giving up on me, at the worst of times.

Prologue

Parts Of Me: A Series of Untamed Words searches for the meaning of life and how it treats humans throughout a lifetime.

Contents

STRUGGLES

Chapter1

Sometimes it's hard to explain
How you feel,
You want to get a hold,
You want to leave too.
You feel choked,
But you also feel some known touches,
You want to sit alone,
But you also want a hand to make yours warm.
You're in a continuous loop,
And it drains you out.
You want to get free,
But you also want to get strangled,
You want to be like the skies,
But you also want to be the stars trapped up there.

Chapter2

I‘m struggling for a breath,
I’m on my own today,
I feel like a burden,
I feel like a dry winter leaf,
Everything around me is in motion,
But I'm as still as a rock.
I put a leg forward,
But I forget about the ropes,
I fall,
And almost get hit by a piece of broken glass.
I lay there for a while,
Until I see my muse,
Until I hear my own voices,
Until my mind reads out my thoughts loud,
Until I don’t hear a sobbing heart and a soul full of wry.

Chapter3

It sucks to feel so much,
Every day becomes a struggle,
Full of questions,
Doubts,
Insecurities,
Misunderstandings,
Emotional baggages,
And what not.
But it's even worse,
When you don't know how to express it.
It gets buried inside of you,
It makes your heart ache,
And it brings out a side of you,
You never knew existed.
I think, I can write it out,
I can be expressive,
I can make people understand me,
But I was wrong.
I can do nothing.
I can never share myself.
I can never be a part of anyone.

Chapter4

Why do I feel left out today?
This feeling is crumbling me down.
This feeling of not being good enough,
This feeling of not knowing enough,
This feeling of lacking skills,
It is killing me today.
I am running in a race,
And I can see the end line,
But I'm not nearing it.
It's a rocky path,
I'm falling,
I'm lagging behind.
I'm losing every hope,
I'm on the verge of giving up,
I want to run and reach the end,
But I don't have the strength.
Is this me just today?
Or is it going to be me all my life?
Am I never going to be good enough?
Am I always going to lose?
Or am I going to win this rat-race?

Chapter5

Don't expect me to be good today,
Don't expect me to shine,
Don't expect me to give you a smile today,
Don't expect me to be fine.
Don't expect me to grow like a blooming flower,
Don't expect me to move on like the flowing river,
Don't expect me to stay calm like the patient sky,
Don't expect me to be kind like the shimmering stars.
I'm like the soil under the grave today,
Weak and tired.
I'm like the stone in the ocean today,
Cold and full of despair.
Maybe just sit beside me,
And see me breathe today.
Won't that be enough for once?

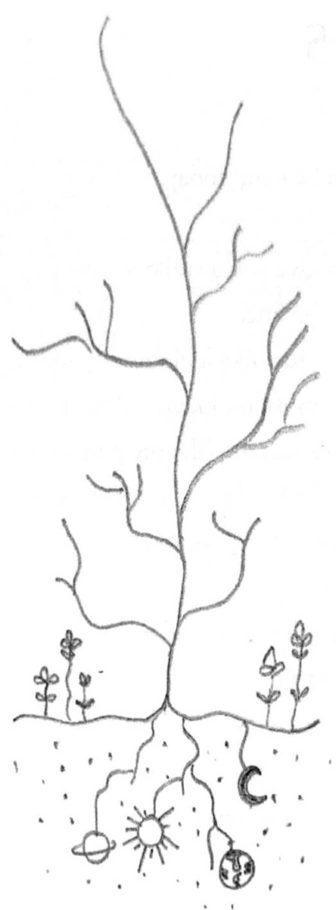

Chapter6

Do you know what chaos looks like?
I didn't know either,
until today.
But I know now.
When you're standing under the shower,
And the water hits your body,
It looks like they plan on killing you,
They rush towards you with all their force,
All their rage,
But you're unaware of it,
You think they're making love to you
You feel them with your eyes closed,
But when you try to look through them,
It aches,
It burns,
You realize it's delusional.
They don't want to soothe you,
They want to rip you apart.
You still stand there,
Unable to gulp down the reality,
And trying to comprehend life.

Chapter7

It's a gloomy evening today,
I didn't hear any birds,
I didn't see the sunset,
I didn't see the moon coming to my window,
I didn't feel the wind.
It's an evening, with no lights,
A lot of screams,
Dreadful fights,
And a pool of tears.
I question myself,
Not just today,
I do it every other day,
Why is this me?
Why do I feel this way?
What causes me pain?
There are no answers to all that,
The only answer I find
When I look at the sky is,
There are a million stars in that gloomy sky,
But not each one of them shines every day.

Chapter8

It's a warm Tuesday morning,
Sunshine, birds, blooming flowers
Especially sunflowers.
Almost looks like a dreamy garden of love.
I look out of the window and the wind brushes my face,
I close my eyes, trying to feel it, instead
All I feel is the touch of a hand,
The touch that I know, and the touch I've been craving for.
I open my eyes in the hope of seeing him,
Right in front of me,
But I don't.
All I see is an empty dull summer morning,
With a rushing wild wind,
And all I feel is
A dark cloud trying to choke me.
It was the presence that I needed,
And it was the goodbye that I had to face.

Chapter9

I'm sinking deep
The pain inside of me is growing,
Getting big,
And is gulping me in.
It's not my fault,
It's not his fault,
We don't know who's responsible,
We don't know why,
We only know that we still have us,
We still have the same love,
We can still hear our hearts beat,
A thousand miles away.

Chapter10

I had bizarre thoughts last night,
Thoughts like death mostly,
Death of my dear ones, as far as I remember.
It felt like a void,
It felt like a stone on my chest,
It felt like a tight rope around my neck,
It felt like someone was banging my door, but I failed to open it.
It was like a sudden gush of emotions,
Sudden feeling of being all alone,
Sudden reminder of not being enough,
Sudden worries of not being able to cope up,
It was every grief at once.
It was a nightmare,
An unforgettable one,
The one I can't say out loud,
But the one that will always roam inside me through unknown paths.

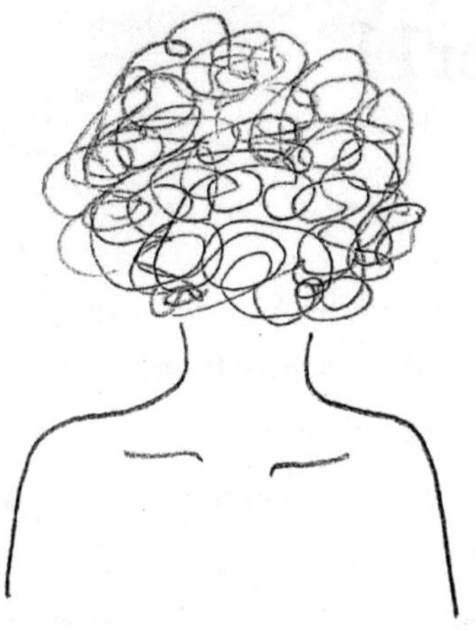

Chapter11

I'm tired.
Tired of looking at people,
Wrapped with all the expensive things,
And pretending to be fine,
When they too are hurt and broken.
I don't hate them,
And the sane me would have been proud of them,
For getting up every day and pretending to be okay, even
When they are not.
But me, right now,
Would like them to take their masks off,
Just for once,
So that I could stand up,
And shout,
That I'm not the only one.

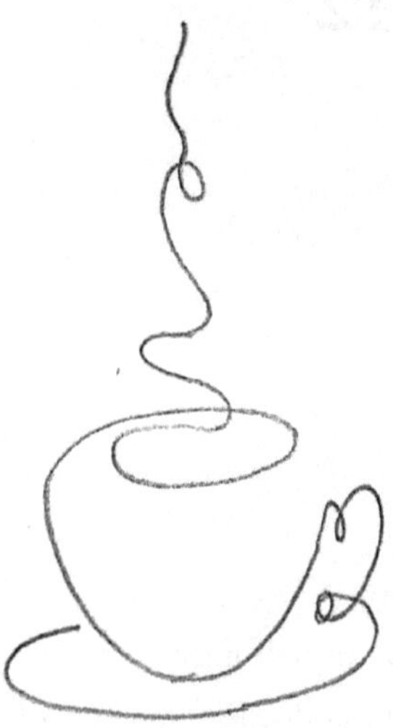

Chapter12

I'm upset,
Angry,
Pissed,
And happy,
Grateful,
Excited.
I'm everything today.
I feel like locking up myself inside a room,
With a bag of snacks and some music,
But I know I'll be bored alone.
I'll need someone to talk to,
And I'll walk in front of the mirror,
And talk to myself.
Not just talk,
I'll cry,
Laugh and even
Fight myself.
Then I'll need a real person,
To talk what I want to talk,
And then,
I would want them to shut up,
And leave.
I'll feel better,

And again alone,
I'll cry myself to sleep,
And think why am I this way.

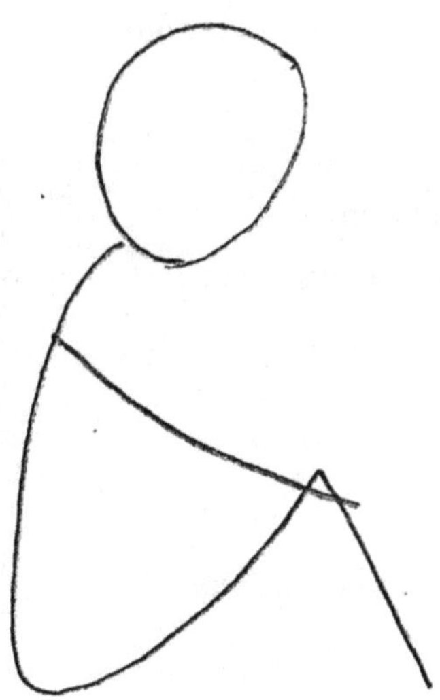

Chapter13

I'm writing to you now,
I'm going numb with each word,
You're meant to find me in each word,
You can't.
I'm still writing,
Holding up each breath,
Hoping that now you might hear,
My cries,
My sorrow,
My grief,
My love,
Through every silent line, I write,
You can't.
I've stopped writing today,
I'll write again,
Maybe tomorrow,
Maybe never.

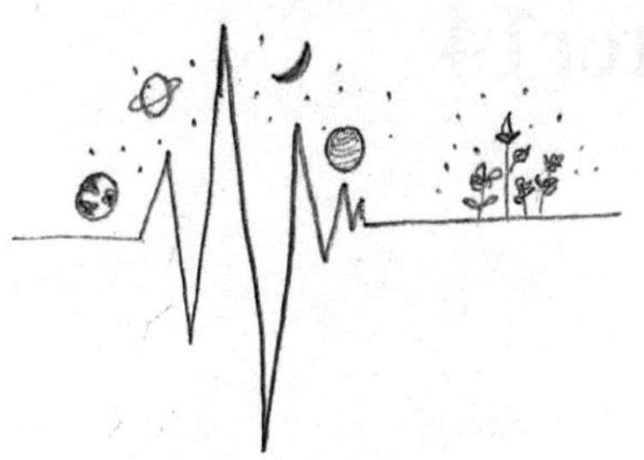

Chapter14

You're scared,
I too am.
You're a difficult mystery,
And I'm bad at solving it.
But I've listened,
Every time you didn't speak.
I've overheard you,
Talking to yourself.
Did I interrupt your
Flow of thoughts?
Did I leave enough space
For your mind?
Or did I just slip in?

Chapter15

I'm not hurt today,
I wasn't hurt yesterday,
Nor the day before it,
But I feel different,
Not excited,
Not heartbroken,
Not full of rage,
It's just different.
I think it doesn't make sense,
But I ask questions, that I shouldn't be asking,
I write things, that I shouldn't be writing,
And I do things, that I shouldn't be doing.
Does that make sense at all?

Chapter16

I'm laying under a rock today,
A rock that breaks me into pieces.
I'm not enough today,
Everything feels like an ending,
Everything is crashing,
Everything is moving, yet standing still.
This is a rock that is taking away my own self.
This rock is telling me to end everything, including myself.
This rock wants me to stop breathing, and lay still.
this rock is putting me into a dilemma.
Some will say, I should not give up and that I should push the rock away.
Some will say, to pretend till the rock gives up on its own.
But I want to give in today,
I want my breath to stop,
I want my body to get cold,
I want my eyes to be wide open,
I want to feel death.

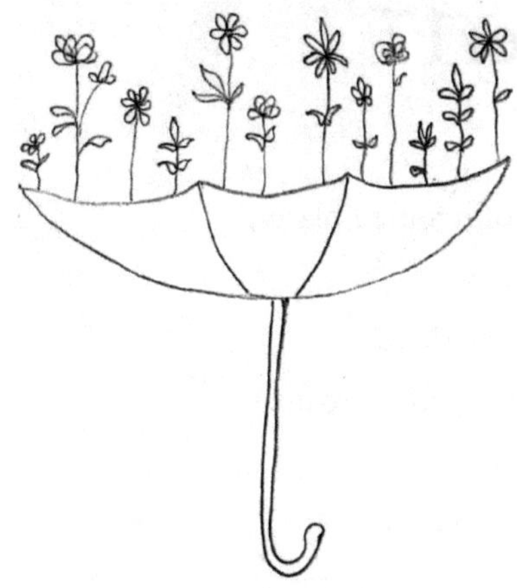

Chapter17

I am not a fan of haunted places,
But I love the dark,
I won't walk alone there,
But I would let my mind roam.
I love the nights,
Not because it's lonely,
But because I like to be in peace.
The peace that comes with it.
It's the same with haunted places,
It's peace, until you let your mind roam.
It's peace in the night too,
When you're staring at the ceiling,
But it's chaos,
Once you let your mind roam,
And your heart scream.

Chapter18

I cut my thumb today
I saw blood dripping
From the finger to the floor
I kept staring at it
Until the floor turned red.
My finger was looking better now
With a cut,
So deep,
Like a stream of red water,
Like the color of lonely nights,
Like the scream of a devil,
All painted by death, for death.

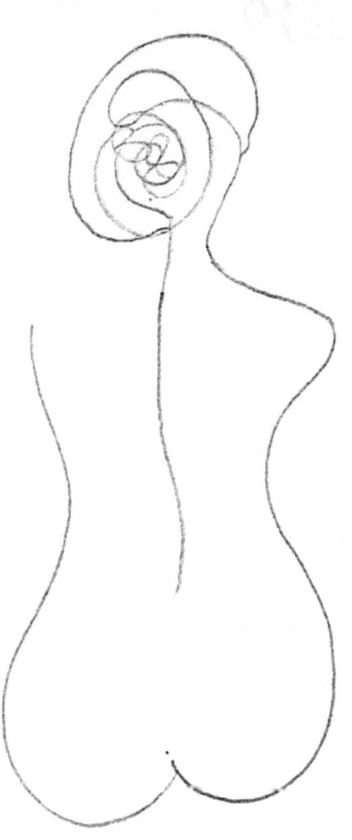

Chapter19

1:45 AM, late night
My pillow is wet,
My nose is red,
My cries don't have a noise,
My head is heavy,
My throat feels like I'm choking,
My hands are shivering,
My feet are cold.
2:00 AM, late night
My Instagram feels like a void,
I've plugged my earphones,
Moonlight getting through the window,
Winds making my curtains flow,
I can hear my fan moving.
3:05 AM, late night
Closing my eyes,
Not sleeping,
Thinking where's the start,
Where's the end,
Wide awake again,
Goosebumps,
More silent tears,
Sudden chest pain,

Aches. More aches.
4:00 AM, almost morning
I want to feel the knife,
I want to feel the pain,
I want to know how much I can bear,
I want to know what's inside me,
I want to know who'll cry if I do so,
I want to see suffering,
I want to see fear.
4:45 AM, morning
I can see blood,
And it has painted me.

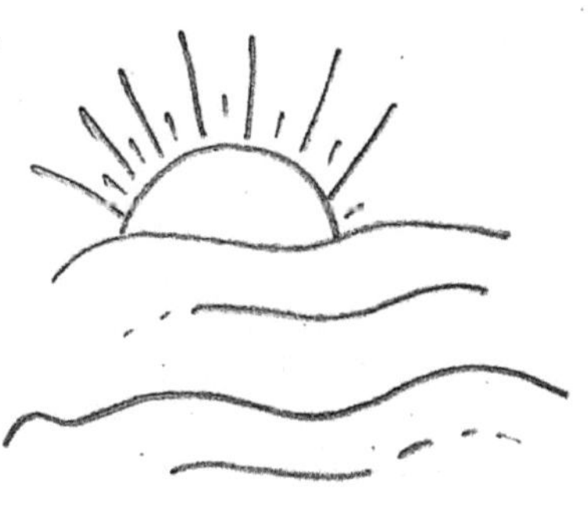

Chapter20

PEACE

Chapter21

Can you catch the wind?
Can you touch the sound of waves?
Can you really smell the earth after some drizzle?
Can you measure the dark blue oceans?
Can you paint the evening sky with a shade of pink every day?
Can you actually talk to the stars and the moon?
Can you hold on to all the shimmering lights?
Can you look at pain?
Can you taste the sweetness of a child's smile?
Can you feel your lover's voice ripping through your body?
Can you mould happiness?
Can you hug life?

Chapter22

When a feeling isn't explainable,
But makes you extraordinarily overwhelmed,
Is that supposed to be love?
I guess so.
I woke up with the sun today,
And wished he was here,
To witness the orange and red hues.
I was having a sandwich for breakfast,
And wished that he could eat with me too,
They're his favorite.
I was reading a book,
And wished that I could read it out to him.
I was clicking random pictures,
And wished I could click pictures of him too.
I woke up again,
But this time the sun wasn't waiting for me,
It was throwing pink and purple shade,
And I wished he was here,
To witness the colours of the sky,
Because he loves sunsets and I love him.

Chapter23

Meet me under this sky,
Take my fears away,
Hold my hand,
And tell me,
You'll always find me,
In this ocean of life.

Chapter24

I sit here at 6 PM,
As the skies turn orange,
Then a bit yellow,
And suddenly ocean blue.
I'm taking pictures
Of the sunsets.
i promise myself,
to come back again,
Tomorrow
For the hopeful sunrise.
Would that be orange,
Yellow,
And suddenly ocean blue?
I doubt.

Chapter25

I wish I knew how to swim.
I could skim on the surface,
Float till infinity,
And find my shore at the very end.
But I can't,
So I choose to drown for you.

Chapter26

Deep smiles surrounding me,
Like an ocean with waves
I'm hiding in between,
Like the little pearls
Flowing,
Looking around,
And searching,
For my own shore.

Chapter27

This sky makes me cry,
Out of joy,
Sadness,
Warmth,
Fear.
It makes me crave,
For life,
For love,
For a you,
And for an us.

Chapter28

I'm burning with emotions tonight,
I'm aflame today,
He has taken control of my soul,
I can't think straight,
I can't talk sense,
All I do is
Blush a little,
Stare at him,
And talk love.
All I know today is that,
This is what I never had,
This is what I always needed,
And this is what I'll crave for my whole life.

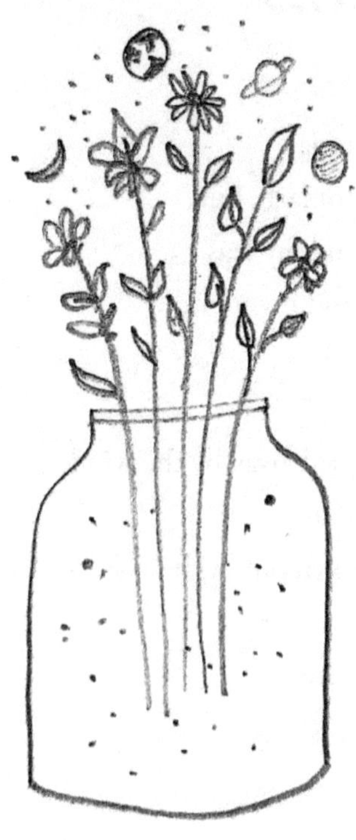

Chapter29

I feel butterflies today,
Not just in my stomach, but
Inside my arms and my legs,
Inside my chest and my mouth.
I feel light,
Like a feather
That is being carried away by the wind,
Like the tiny raindrops
That is being thrown out of the sky.
I feel I can fly.
Fly because I feel free,
I feel loved,
I feel warm,
I feel close.
You're the reason,
You're the feeling I feel today,
You're here, inside me,
Touching inch by inch,
Making sure not a single part is left unloved.

Chapter30

Walking with the wind,
His hair flying,
Like a lonely leaf.
His rigid hands following,
Like a flowing river.
He looks back,
His eyes revolving like the sun,
His face shimmering like stars,
His smile fascinating like the moon,
His body, dark and strong like the clouds.
He looks back again,
His hands touching mine,
I didn't know he feels like my pillow,
Soft and warm.
I'm breathing his breath right now,
And I just realized,
He feels like my ice cream too,
Sweet and smooth.

Chapter31

It's turning blue,
The night sky is welcoming the stars,
As I lay here,
Gazing,
Listening,
Thinking,
A star falls by,
I close my eyes,
And wish for you.

Chapter32

It starts and ends with me for you.

-Sometimes it's hard to express what you feel and how you feel. You get impatient trying to find the apt words for it. So you decide to converse in the words of your heart, and when you do, you spill rawness, you spill magic and you spill your golden love.

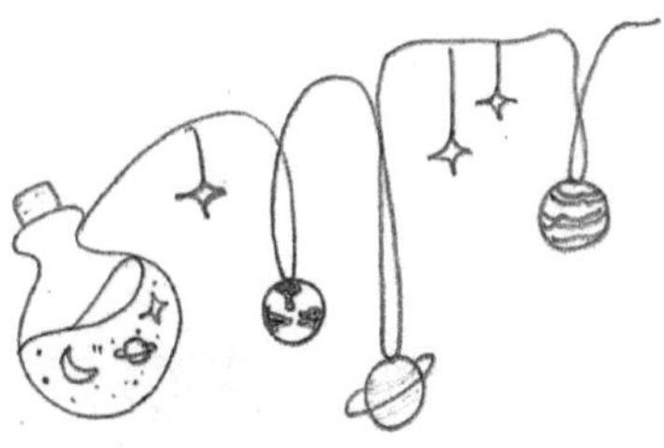

Chapter33

Some poetries rip your heart,
Some poetries get to your bones and veins,
Some poetries sit inside your head,
Some poetries flow through your blood,
Some poetries make you,
And some poetries are you.

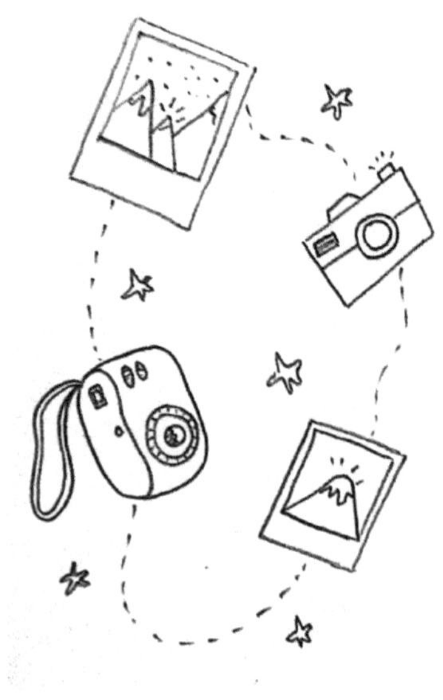

Chapter34

STORIES

Chapter35

I just read something, that hurt me, made me want to question everything, drew some boundaries, and made me feel sick.

What do you do when you lose faith? All the faith you had in all the love you gave, all the efforts you made, all the confessions you did, all the time you had given, all the fears that you faced. What do you do?

They leave. One fine day, when the skies turn blue-grey, and the winds blow from north to south and you sit under the stars, they leave. You can't bear it, you run, you beg, cry, but they, leave.

You lock yourself inside that dark room you have, without windows and just ventilators. You are filled with different emotions, a lot of pain, and a little bit of contentment, remembering that you tried till the very end. But the sadness is more powerful and it engulfs you, bit by bit. You sit in a corner, with folded hands, and thinking about all the times they said they won't leave, of all the times when they assured their love, of all the times they said they valued you. You still want to believe them. You tell yourself a story. You tell yourself they still love you and it's their way of testing your love, or maybe they are going through something worse than you. You think of seeing sunlight today, you walk to the door and you hear a knock, you struggle to open it, but your shivering hands do it anyway. There he is, standing right outside that door. How did he know you were hiding from reality in that tiny room? Did his instincts tell him? Or his love for you? You want to hold him, and tell him how long have you waited, but your mouth doesn't allow you to say a word. You stand there, staring at him, like a stone, carved in a human form. After a moment of silence, he speaks with his deep voice that you always liked and says: I want you to meet her. And there she is, the one he always talked about, the one you saw in all his meetings and his outings. His face breaks into a nervous smile, you've longed to see this. But then, he looks at her and she smiles her brightest smile. You can't figure out if you loved him more than her or not. You take a few steps back, hold the doorknob, and shut it.

You're locked inside, one more time.

Chapter36

There are days when you isolate yourself from the outside world. You find yourself a little corner and sit there inside your mind, thinking and counting each breath that comes out of you. You feel empty yet so heavy with all the burden. You try to be calm but you're all chaos inside. You roll yourself up into a ball of restlessness. Every drop that flows down your eyes adds to your sea of grief. You crawl and stand in front of the mirror, and look yourself in the eyes. You pinch yourself to feel the pain, but you don't feel it. You bite yourself and scratch yourself, it still doesn't hurt. You scream, and it's not the pain but the numbness that hurts.

You suddenly stop and crawl back to your corner and rest your head on your knees. Your eyes see the moon through the window and they fill up with tears again. Again, it's not the pain that hurts, but the imperfections of the moon and the darkness of the clouds and the impatience of the stars that humans find so alluring. You feel their pain, you feel their scars, and then you feel their strength.

You get up, walk to the window and the moonlight brightens up your gloomy room.

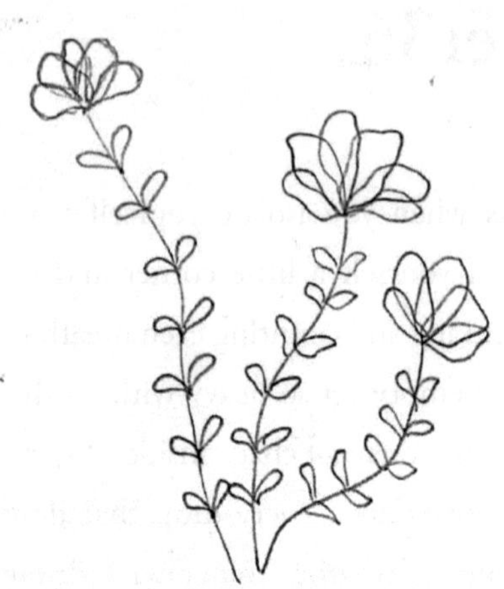

Chapter37

CONFESSION

Chapter38

It's been a year or two,
Of holding grudges,
Of blaming people,
Of being petrified
Of touches.
It's bone tingling,
To even think.
It's heartbreaking,
When your own people
Turn out to be demons,
Of filthy desires.
It was a warm morning,
With the sun glowing
At its brightest.
I was on my way home,
Looking away from reality,
Into the field of love, hope and kindness,
And suddenly I felt shivers,
All over my body,
As I felt his hand,
On my chest,
Trying to feel me,
And pretending it was fine.

I couldn't face him,
I couldn't form a smile,
I could only get terrified
I could only stare with stone eyes,
I could only feel the hurt,
I could only let my tears flow.
My train reached home,
I saw my dad,
Waiting for me,
Smiling at me,
I tried,
To smile,
But I don't know
If I did.
I ran,
Without a word,
Held his hand,
And held my breath,
Till I reached my mom.

-This is not fiction. This was me, three years back, when I was coming home with one of my family friends, whom I've known for years, since my childhood, and he, out of everyone tried to molest me. I first thought, I was only being stupid and that he can never do something like that, but there's a feeling that reaches your stomach and your bones and makes you puke and shiver till you cry and get numb. It was one of those feelings. I kept it with me, but today when I look back at it, I feel I should've stood up against it and opened up to people, but I didn't then. I blamed myself, for not reacting all this while, so I thought of finally letting it go by letting it out. Note: Open up as soon as possible, and don't let the devils ruin your life. You're stronger than you think.

Chapter39

THANK YOU FOR SUPPORTING ME THROUGH EVERYTHING

MOM

DAD

BONU

SOUMIK

Chapter40

This is my first ever book, and I'm grateful to each one of you who has been a part of this beautiful journey. Thank you for supporting me and pushing me. Thank you for pointing out my faults and helping me get better. For making me realize my mistakes and work on them. Thank you for being my biggest critic and my constant supporter. You all are gems!

I hope each one of you will find a piece of yourself in this compilation of heartbreaking and heartwarming poems. May you find your solace and peace in this mini-book. Happy reading, keep reading, and spreading love.

Thank you!

To, my family,

I wouldn't have reached here without you. Thank you for believing in me. Though there were times when I got scolded for doing things other than studying but eventually I ended up doing what I wanted to.

9 798886 843446

Printed by Libri Plureos GmbH in Hamburg,
Germany